100 SOLOS
SAXOPHONE

Amsco Publications
London/New York/Sydney

Order No. AM 33705
International Standard Book Number: 0.8256.1099.0

Exclusive Distributors:
Music Sales Corporation
257 Park Avenue South, New York, NY 10010
Music Sales Limited
8/9 Frith Street, London W1V 5TZ England
Music Sales Pty. Limited
120 Rothschild Street, Rosebery, Sydney, NSW 2018, Australia

Printed in the United States of America by
Vicks Lithograph and Printing Corporation

AS LONG AS HE NEEDS ME (FROM THE COLUMBIA PICTURES-ROMULUS FILM "OLIVER").

Words and Music by Lionel Bart.

Moderato

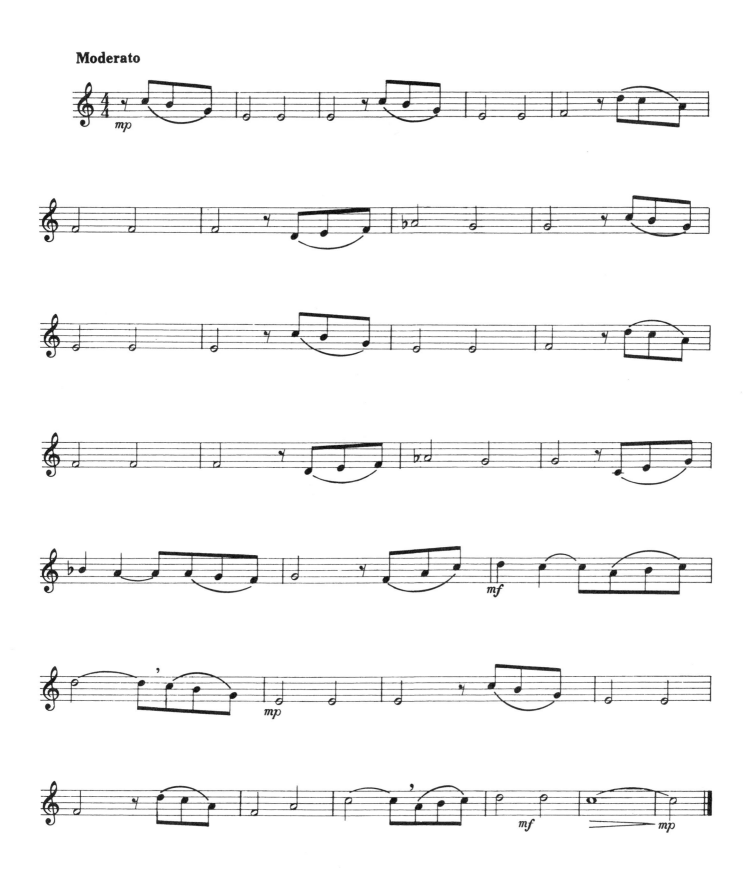

STEPTOE AND SON.
Music by Ron Grainer.

Moderato

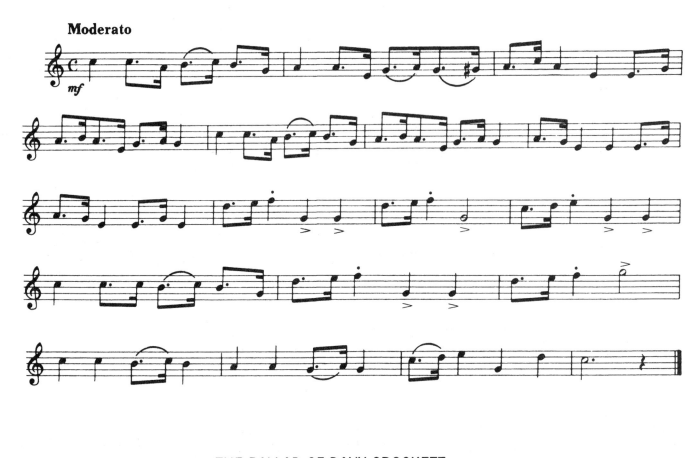

THE BALLAD OF DAVY CROCKETT.
Words by Tom Blackburn. Music by George Burns.

Moderato

ENGLISH DANCE.

by J.C. Bach.

Allegretto

LITTLE BOXES.
Words and Music by Malvina Reynolds.

Moderate Waltz Tempo

MORNING HAS BROKEN.

Traditional.

Moderato

OOM-PAH-PAH (FROM THE COLUMBIA PICTURES-ROMULUS FILM "OLIVER").

Words and Music by Lionel Bart.

PENNY LANE.

Words and Music by John Lennon and Paul McCartney.

Moderately Bright

REVIEWING THE SITUATION (FROM THE COLUMBIA PICTURES-ROMULUS FILM "OLIVER").

Words and Music by Lionel Bart.

SERENADE.

by Franz Schubert.

Moderato

SGT. PEPPER'S LONELY HEARTS CLUB BAND.

Words and Music by John Lennon and Paul McCartney.

BIBBIDI-BOBBIDI-BOO.

Words by Jerry Livingston. Music by Mack David and Al Hoffman.

Light Schottische tempo

CONSIDER YOURSELF (FROM THE COLUMBIA PICTURES-ROMULUS FILM "OLIVER").

Words and Music by Lionel Bart.

March tempo

LOVE ME TENDER.
Words and Music by Elvis Presley and Vera Matson.

Moderately slow

ENGLISH COUNTRY GARDEN.
Traditional.

Moderato

STRAWBERRY FIELDS FOREVER.

Words and Music by John Lennon and Paul McCartney.

Moderato

WHEN I'M SIXTY-FOUR.

Words and Music by John Lennon and Paul McCartney.

Medium bounce

WHO WILL BUY (FROM THE COLUMBIA PICTURES-ROMULUS FILM "OLIVER").

Words and Music by Lionel Bart.

WHO DO YOU THINK YOU'RE KIDDING, MR. HITLER?

Words by Jimmy Perry. Music by Jimmy Perry and Derek Taverner.

WHERE IS LOVE (FROM THE COLUMBIA PICTURES-ROMULUS FILM "OLIVER").

Words and Music by Lionel Bart.

MICHELLE.
Words and Music by John Lennon and Paul McCartney.

SHE'S LEAVING HOME.

Words and Music by John Lennon and Paul McCartney.

Moderato

YELLOW SUBMARINE.

Words and Music by John Lennon and Paul McCartney.

Moderately bright

WALTZ.
by Johannes Brahms.

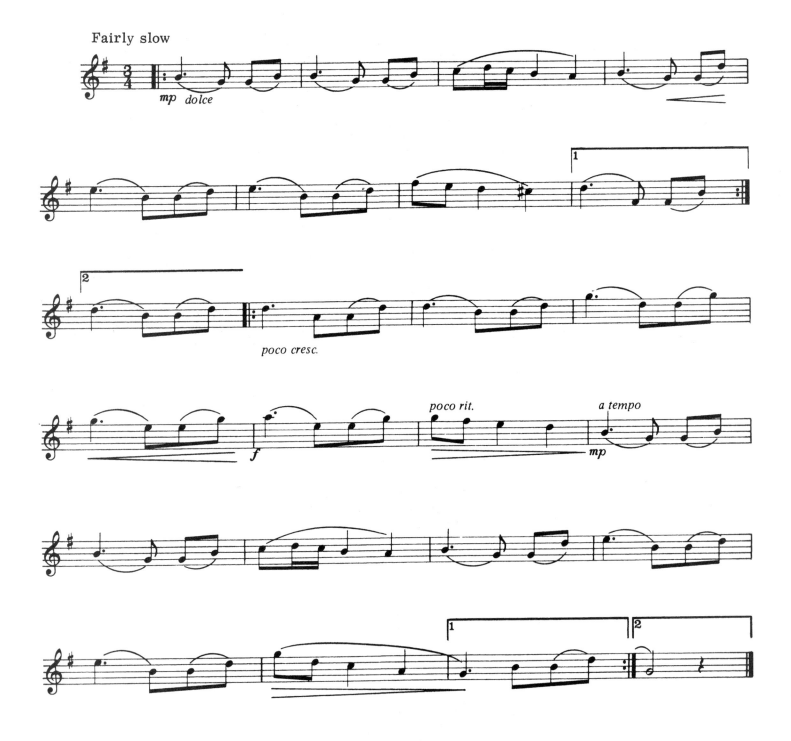

CHIM CHIM CHER-EE.
Words and Music by Richard M. Sherman and Robert B. Sherman.

25

CAROLINA MOON.

Words by Benny Davis. Music by Joe Burke.

BLUESETTE.

Words by Norman Gimbel. Music by John Thielemans.

Moderate waltz tempo

SCARBOROUGH FAIR.
Traditional.

Moderately slow

SMILE.

Words by John Turner and Geoffrey Parsons. Music by Charles Chaplin.

Andante

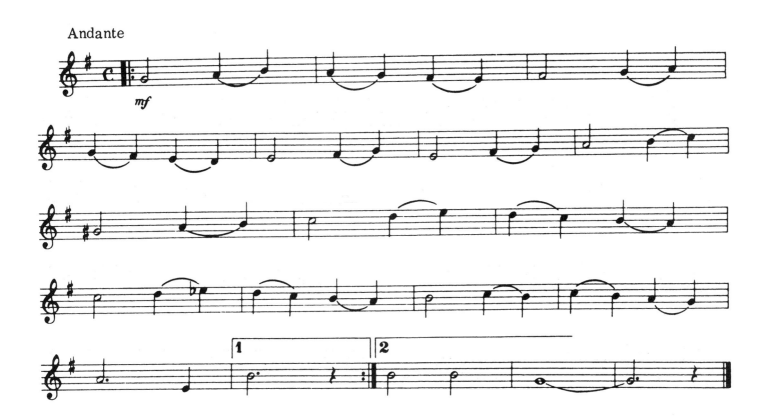

IT'S NOT UNUSUAL.

Words and Music by Gordon Mills & Les Reed.

Moderately, with a beat

YOU'RE THE DEVIL IN DISGUISE.

Words and Music by Bill Grant, Bernie Baum and Florence Kaye.

MONEY, MONEY, MONEY.

Words and Music by Benny Andersson and Bjorn Ulvaeus.

Moderato

PICK A POCKET OR TWO.

Words and Music by Lionel Bart.

A DREAM.
by Peter I. Tchaikovsky.

Moderato

BOURÉE.

by George Frederic Handel.

Moderato

MERRY DANCE.

by Rameau.

MINUET.

by George Frederic Handel.

Moderato

ROMANCE.
by Ludwig van Beethoven.

SCOTTISH DANCE.

by Ludwig van Beethoven.

Moderately fast

BIRDIE SONG BIRDIE DANCE.

Words and Music by Werner Thomas and Terry Randall.

MARY'S BOY CHILD.

Words and Music by Jester Hairston.

WHITE ROSE OF ATHENS.

Music by Manos Hadjidakis. Words by Norman Newell.
Additional Words by Archie Bleyer.

GETTING TO KNOW YOU (FROM "THE KING AND I").

Words by Oscar Hammerstein. Music by Oscar Hammerstein.

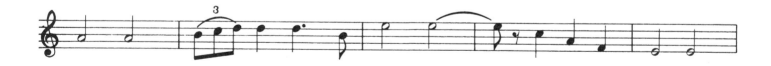

JEANIE WITH THE LIGHT BROWN HAIR.

by Steven Foster.

IMAGINE.

Words and Music by John Lennon.

Moderato

LILLYWHITE.
Words and Music by Cat Stevens.

Moderato

NORWEGIAN WOOD.

Words and Music by John Lennon and Paul McCartney.

Slowly

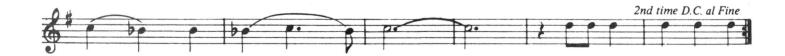

STRANGERS IN THE NIGHT.

Words by Charles Singleton and Eddie Snyder. Music by Bert Kaempfert.

Moderately slow

YOU NEVER DONE IT LIKE THAT.

Words and Music by Neil Sedaka and Howard Greenfield.

THEME FROM A SUMMER PLACE.

Words by Mack Discant. Music by Max Steiner.

BYE BYE BABY.

Words and Music by Leo Robin and Jule Styne.

Moderato

THE ENTERTAINER.
by Scott Joplin.

WITH A LITTLE HELP FROM MY FRIENDS.

Words and Music by John Lennon and Paul McCartney.

BRING ME SUNSHINE.

Words by Sylvia Dee. Music by Arthur Kent.

With an easy swing

ALL SHOOK UP.

Words and Music by Otis Blackwell and Elvis Presley.

Medium rock

BLUE SUEDE SHOES.

Words and Music by Carl Lee Perkins.

Bright tempo

HOW CAN I TELL YOU.

Words and Music by Cat Stevens.

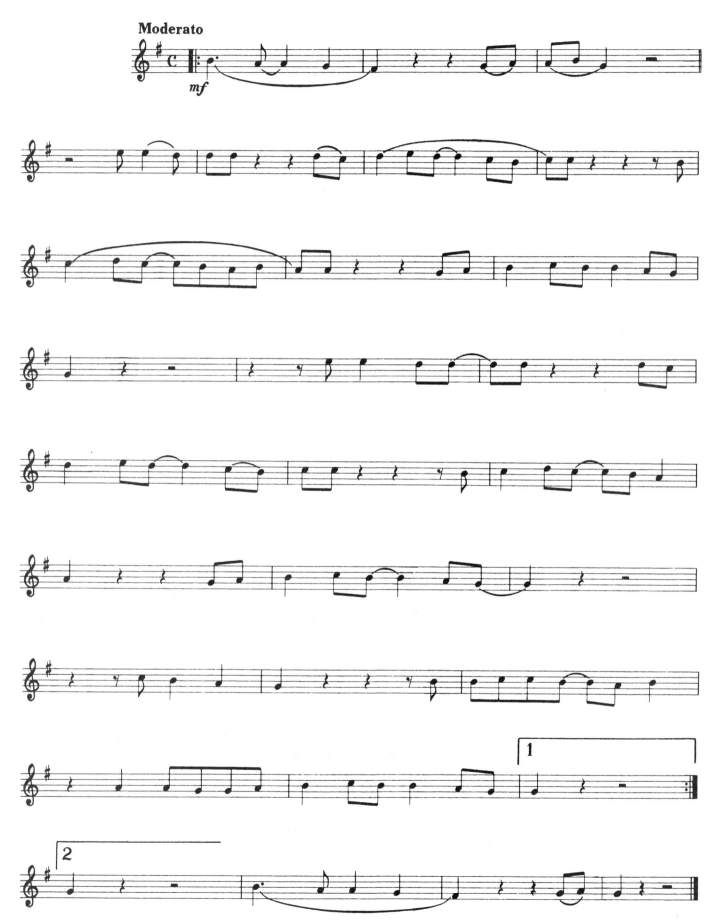

I'D LIKE TO TEACH THE WORLD TO SING.

Words and Music by Roger Cook, Roger Greenaway, Billy Backer and Billy Davis.

Moderato

D.S. al Fine

EDELWEISS (FROM "THE SOUND OF MUSIC").

Words by Oscar Hammerstein II. Music by Richard Rodgers.

Slowly, with expression

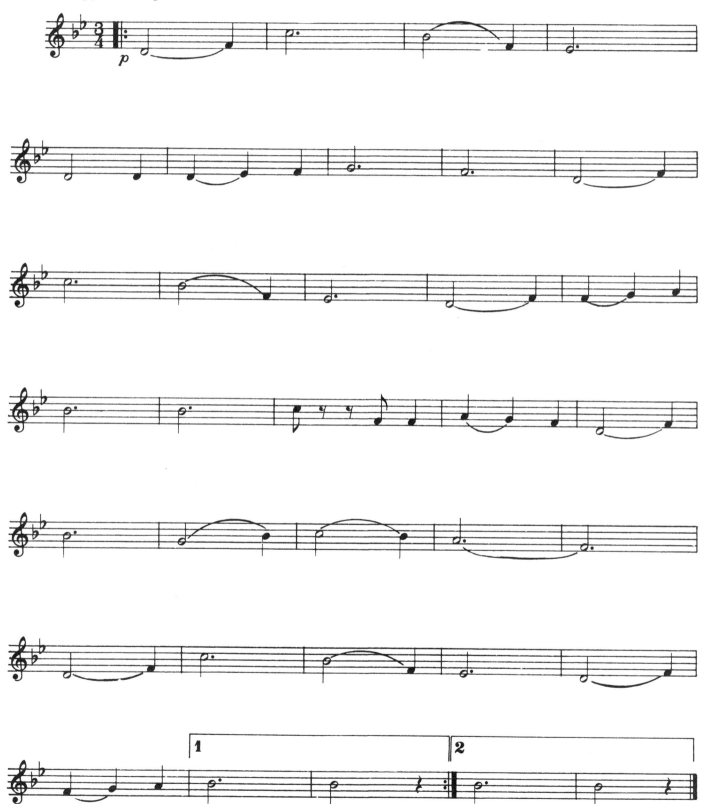

DAYS OF WINE AND ROSES.

Words by Johnny Mercer. Music by Henry Mancini.

Moderato

WHEN THE SAINTS GO MARCHING IN.

Traditional.

SAILING.
Words and Music by Gavin Sutherland.

Slow Beat

MONA BONE JAKON.

Words and Music by Cat Stevens.

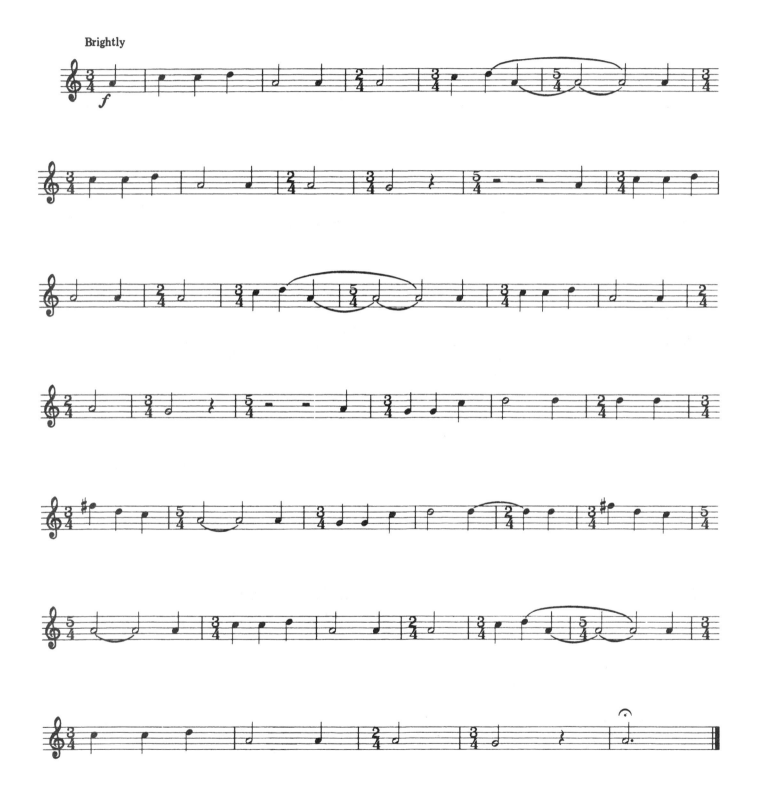

ON WINGS OF SONG.

by Felix Mendelssohn.

ANDANTINO (TRIO FROM WALTZ, OP. 19).

by Franz Schubert.

CAN CAN.
by Jacques Offenbach.

NOCTURNE (FROM SECOND STRING QUARTET).

by Alexander Borodin.

ERIE CANAL.
Traditional.

Moderato
Piano

PRELUDE TO THE AFTERNOON OF A FAUN.

by Claude Debussy.

SONATA.
by Johannes Brahms.

POET AND PEASANT OVERTURE.

by Franz Von Suppe.

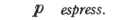

PASSING BY.

by Edward Purcell.

Andantino

MARCH (FROM "LOVE OF THREE ORANGES").

by Serge Prokofieff.

Tempo di Marcia

KOMM, SÜSSER TOD.

by J.S. Bach.

Andante

MARCH OF THE TOYS (FROM "BABES IN TOYLAND").

by Victor Herbert.

MAPLE LEAF RAG.

by Scott Joplin.

Medium bounce

MINUET.

by Ludwig van Beethoven.

MORNING (FROM "PEER GYNT SUITE").
by Edvard Grieg.

REVERIE.
by Claude Debussy.

Andantino

RONDE DES PRINCESSES (FROM "THE FIREBIRD SUITE").

by Igor Stravinsky.

POLKA (FROM "THE BARTERED BRIDE").

by Bedrich Smetana.

SWAN LAKE.
by Peter I. Tchaikovsky.

THEME FROM "SYMPHONY IN D MINOR".

by Cesar Franck.

ADIOS MUCHACHOS.

by Carlos Sanders.

LA CUMPARSITA.

by G.H. Matos Rodrigues.

AFTER THE BALL.

Charles K. Harris.

Moderato

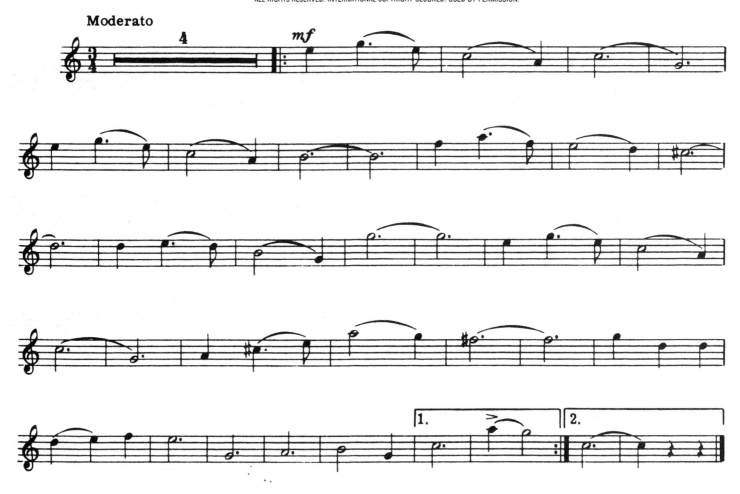

SANTA LUCIA.

Neapolitan Song.

Andantino

THE BAND PLAYED ON.

by Charles E. Ward.

Tempo di Valse

AH, SO PURE (FROM "MARTHA").

by Friedrich Von Flotow.

AMERICAN PATROL.
by F.W. Meacham.

BATTLE HYMN OF THE REPUBLIC.
by Julia Ward Howe.

FANTASIE IMPROMPTU, OP. 66 (THEME).
by Frederic Chopin.

MEXICAN HAT DANCE.

by F.A. Partichella.

FÜR ELISE.

by Ludwig van Beethoven.

TO A WILD ROSE.
by Edward MacDowell.

THE GLOW WORM.
by Paul Lincke.

Tempo di Gavotte

EL CHOCLO.
by A.G. Villoldo.

O SOLE MIO.

by E. DiCapua.

RED RIVER VALLEY.

Cowboy Song.

LA PALOMA.
by Sebastian Yradier.